# MAKING MONEY WITH TIKTOK

Go Viral, Get Noticed and
Boost Your Brand Presence

Genevieve Velzian

Copyright © 2024 Genevieve Velzian

All rights reserved

Any recommendations or opinions given are the author's own and in no way represent a legal point of view. The author accepts no liability for recommendations given.

No part of this book may be reproduced, or stored in a retrieval system, or transmitted in any form or by any means, electronic, mechanical, photocopying, recording, or otherwise, without express written permission of the publisher.

# CONTENTS

| | |
|---|---|
| Title Page | |
| Copyright | |
| Introduction | 1 |
| How to Get Seen | 5 |
| Product Video Ideas | 13 |
| Fun Video Ideas | 29 |
| Influencer Video Ideas | 44 |
| Company Vision Video Ideas | 55 |
| Business Advice TikTok Videos | 66 |
| LifeHacks Video Ideas | 77 |
| How to Have Banter | 86 |
| Allocating Social Media Budget | 92 |
| Filming and Photography | 99 |
| Why Not Instagram? | 105 |
| Dealing with Negativity | 111 |
| Future Trends | 118 |
| Conclusion | 127 |

| Essential Resources | 131 |
| The End | 139 |

# INTRODUCTION

In the digital age, the power of social media platforms cannot be overstated. Among these platforms, TikTok has emerged as a dominant force, capturing the attention of millions worldwide with its unique blend of creativity, entertainment, and rapid content consumption.

With over a billion active users, TikTok offers unparalleled opportunities for brands and individuals alike to reach a vast and engaged audience. Whether you're a budding entrepreneur, a small business owner, or a marketer looking to expand your brand's reach, TikTok is a goldmine waiting to be tapped.

The key to TikTok's success lies in its ability to create viral content. Unlike traditional marketing channels, TikTok thrives on authenticity, creativity, and the unexpected. Videos can gain traction rapidly, reaching millions within hours, sometimes even minutes.

This virality is not just a stroke of luck; it's a blend of art and science, understanding the platform's dynamics, and leveraging its features to your advantage.

**Why TikTok?**

TikTok stands out from other social media platforms due to its unique algorithm and user engagement. The algorithm is designed to surface content that resonates with users, making it possible for anyone to go viral, regardless of their follower count. This democratization of content visibility means that a well-crafted video can propel your product into the spotlight, generating immense interest and driving sales.

Moreover, TikTok's user base is diverse and spans various demographics, making it an ideal platform to connect with a wide range of audiences. From Gen Z to Millennials and beyond, TikTok users are highly engaged, spending significant amounts of time on the platform daily. This high engagement rate provides an excellent opportunity for brands to build relationships with potential customers and foster brand loyalty.

**The Goal of This Book**

This book is designed to be your ultimate guide to creating viral TikTok content that not only captures attention but also drives sales and builds your brand. We will explore a plethora of creative video ideas that can help you showcase your products in the most engaging and effective ways possible. From unboxing videos and customer testimonials to behind-the-scenes looks and trending challenges, this book covers a wide range of content types that can help your brand stand out on TikTok.

Each chapter will delve into different strategies and video ideas, providing you with a comprehensive toolkit to kickstart your TikTok journey. You'll learn how to tap into trends, create relatable content, and leverage TikTok's unique features to maximize your reach and engagement.

**The Art of Virality**

Going viral on TikTok is both an art and a science. It requires creativity, timing, and a deep understanding of the platform's culture and trends. While there's no guaranteed formula for virality, certain elements can significantly increase your chances of creating hit content. This includes using popular sounds and hashtags, participating in challenges, and crafting compelling narratives that resonate with viewers.

Throughout this book, we will explore these elements in detail, offering practical tips and insights to help you create content that not only captures attention but also drives meaningful engagement. We'll also highlight success stories and case studies of brands that have mastered the art of TikTok, providing you with real-world examples and inspiration.

**Your Journey Starts Here**

Embarking on your TikTok journey may seem daunting at first, but with the right strategies and a creative mindset, you can turn this platform into a powerful marketing tool for your brand. This book is here to guide you every step of the way, offering actionable ideas and insights to help you navigate the ever-evolving world of TikTok.

So, whether you're a TikTok novice or a seasoned user looking to refine your strategy, this book has something for everyone. Get ready to dive into the exciting world of TikTok, unleash your creativity, and discover the incredible potential of going viral.

Let's get started!

# HOW TO GET SEEN

Creating compelling content is only half the battle when it comes to going viral on TikTok. To truly maximize your reach, you need to understand how to get your videos seen by as many people as possible. This chapter will explore the key strategies and techniques that can help boost your visibility on the platform, leveraging TikTok's algorithm, trends, and community features.

**Understanding TikTok's Algorithm**

TikTok's algorithm plays a crucial role in determining which videos are shown to users. Unlike other social media platforms, TikTok's algorithm is designed to surface content that resonates with users, regardless of the creator's follower count. Here's how you can leverage this algorithm to your advantage:

Engagement is Key: The algorithm prioritizes videos with high engagement rates. This includes likes, comments, shares, and watch time. Create content that encourages interaction. Ask questions, include calls to action, and engage with your audience in the comments.

Watch Time Matters: The longer users watch your video, the better. Create content that captures attention within the first few seconds and keeps viewers hooked until the end. Use engaging visuals, dynamic editing, and compelling storytelling to maintain interest.

Use Trending Sounds and Hashtags: TikTok's algorithm favors videos that use popular sounds and hashtags. Keep an eye on trending sounds and incorporate them into your videos. Similarly, use relevant and trending hashtags to increase the discoverability of your content.

Consistency Pays Off: Regular posting can improve your visibility. Aim to post consistently, whether it's daily or a few times a week. The more content you create, the more opportunities you have to reach a wider audience.

High-Quality Content: While TikTok is known for its casual and spontaneous content, high-quality videos still perform better. Ensure good lighting, clear audio, and steady camera work. Editing your videos to make them visually appealing can also make a significant difference.

**Leveraging Trends and Challenges**

TikTok is a trend-driven platform. Participating in trends and challenges can significantly boost your visibility and engagement. Here's how to stay on top of the latest trends:

Follow Trending Pages: Regularly check the "Discover" page to see what's trending. Follow popular creators and TikTok influencers who often set trends. Participating in trending challenges can put your content in front of a larger audience.

Use Trending Hashtags: Incorporate trending hashtags into your video descriptions. This can help your content get discovered by users who are following or searching for those trends.

Create Your Own Challenge: If you have a unique idea, create your own challenge. Encourage your followers and other users to participate. Make sure your challenge is fun, easy to replicate, and engaging.

Adapt Trends to Your Niche: Not all trends will align with your brand or product. Adapt trends to fit your niche. For example, if a dance challenge is trending, find a way to incorporate your product into the dance.

**Engaging with the TikTok Community**

Building a community on TikTok is essential for long-term success. Engaging with your audience can increase your visibility and foster loyalty. Here's how to effectively engage with the TikTok community:

Respond to Comments: Take the time to respond to comments on your videos. Engaging with your audience can build a sense of community and encourage more interaction.

Collaborate with Other Creators: Partnering with other TikTok creators can help you reach new audiences. Look for creators who share your interests or have a similar follower base.

Go Live: Use TikTok's live streaming feature to interact with your audience in real-time. Live sessions can increase your visibility and help you build a stronger connection with your followers.

User-Generated Content: Encourage your followers to create content featuring your product. Repost their videos on your profile to show appreciation and build a sense of community.

**Optimising Your Profile**

Your profile is your brand's home on TikTok. Optimize it to attract and retain followers. Here's how:

Profile Picture and Bio: Use a clear, recognizable profile picture. Write a concise, engaging bio that tells users what your brand is about. Include a call to action, like a link to your website or a special promotion.

Links and Contact Information: Take advantage of the space in your bio to include important links, such as your website, other social media profiles, or a link to purchase your product.

Content Organization: Use TikTok's playlist feature to organize your videos into categories. This makes it easier for new followers to find content relevant to their interests.

**Utilising Paid Promotions**

While organic reach on TikTok can be powerful, don't overlook the potential of paid promotions. TikTok offers various advertising options that can boost your visibility:

In-Feed Ads: These are short video ads that appear in users' feeds, blending seamlessly with organic content. Make sure your ads are engaging and align with your brand's voice.

Branded Hashtag Challenges: Create a branded challenge and promote it through TikTok's advertising platform. This can drive massive engagement and visibility.

TopView Ads: These ads appear when users first open the app, guaranteeing high visibility. Use this feature to promote new products or important announcements.

Influencer Partnerships: Partner with TikTok influencers to reach a wider audience. Influencers can create authentic content that resonates with their followers, driving interest and engagement in your product.

**Analysing Performance**

To continually improve your TikTok strategy, regularly analyse your performance. Use TikTok's analytics tools to track key metrics:

View and Engagement Rates: Monitor the number of views, likes, comments, and shares your videos receive. High engagement rates indicate that your content resonates with your audience.

Follower Growth: Track your follower count over time. A steady increase suggests that your content is attracting new viewers.

Audience Insights: Understand your audience's demographics, including age, gender, and location. This can help you tailor your content to better meet their interests and preferences.

Performance Trends: Identify which types of content perform best. Use this insight to inform your future content strategy, focusing on what works and iterating on what doesn't.

**Conclusion**

Getting your videos seen on TikTok requires a mix of creativity, consistency, and strategic engagement. By understanding TikTok's algorithm, leveraging trends and challenges, engaging with the community, optimising your profile, utilising paid promotions, and analysing performance, you can significantly boost your visibility and set the stage for viral success.

Remember, the key to TikTok is to be authentic, stay relevant, and continuously engage with your audience. With these strategies in hand, you're well on your way to making your mark on TikTok and driving meaningful growth for your brand.

# PRODUCT VIDEO IDEAS

If you have a physical product, then the ideas for promoting it in videos are endless. In a way, you're much luckier than a service-based business, because you have something tangible that you can show and use in a video, rather than just having to explain the benefits.

Saying that, you don't want endless cheesy videos of you just talking to the camera, trying to sell your product. Remember that TikTok is SOCIAL media, not just a place to sell. People want to feel like they're being social on when they're on the platform, and they want brands to come across as sociable and friendly as well.

Keeping your channel varied and having a range of different video types requires imagination. Or it requires a pre-made list that I've put together for you.

Here are 200 video ideas for promoting your product on TikTok:

Unboxing your product.

How to use your product.

Before and after using your product.

Customer testimonials.

Behind-the-scenes of product creation.

Day in the life of your team.

Packaging orders for customers.

Common mistakes when using your product.

Product hacks and tips.

User-generated content reposts.

Comparisons with competitors.

Explaining the benefits of your product.

Announcing a sale or promotion.

Introducing a new product.

Q&A about your product.

Partnering with influencers.

Sharing customer reviews.

Creative ways to use your product.

Seasonal uses for your product.

Trending challenges with your product.

Showcasing product features.

Hosting a giveaway.

Product bloopers.

Responding to customer questions.

Time-lapse of product creation.

Sharing your brand story.

Team introductions.

Celebrating company milestones.

User testimonials in action.

Explaining the science behind your product.

Collaborations with other brands.

Demonstrating product durability.

Unique places to use your product.

Highlighting sustainable practices.

How to style your product.

TikTok dances with your product.

ASMR unboxing.

Customer reaction videos.

Explaining the inspiration behind your product.

Showing your product in different settings.

Highlighting limited edition items.

Explaining shipping and returns.

Doing product givebacks or charity.

Offering tips on product maintenance.

Fun facts about your product.

Explaining how to order.

Showcasing DIY projects using your product.

Sharing user-generated art.

Time-lapse of product setup.

Product vs. expectations.

Quick and easy tutorials.

Showcasing multi-functional uses.

Explaining your brand's mission.

Highlighting best-sellers.

Memes involving your product.

Showing products in extreme conditions.

Creative product photography.

Demonstrating product safety.

Highlighting customer transformations.

Sharing customer journey stories.

How to customize your product.

Explaining return on investment.

Showcasing eco-friendly packaging.

Sharing fun facts about your industry.

Product-related trivia.

Explaining industry trends.

Hosting live product demos.

Highlighting community involvement.

Offering exclusive sneak peeks.

Explaining quality control processes.

Showcasing handmade elements.

Partnering with micro-influencers.

Hosting a product countdown.

Sharing user-generated DIY projects.

Product repair tutorials.

Hosting a virtual tour of your workspace.

Explaining your product's development.

Sharing user-generated lifestyle content.

Demonstrating product assembly.

Highlighting your brand values.

Offering limited-time discounts.

Showing your product in travel scenarios.

Sharing product maintenance tips.

Highlighting customer loyalty rewards.

Explaining product warranty.

Showcasing seasonal products.

Sharing behind-the-scenes of product design.

Highlighting unique product features.

Explaining manufacturing processes.

Showing product in action during events.

Offering exclusive content for followers.

Sharing product-themed playlists.

Product care and cleaning tips.

Demonstrating product versatility.

Highlighting user-generated content from events.

Sharing testimonials from industry experts.

Hosting product-themed games.

Explaining your brand's impact.

Sharing success stories.

Demonstrating product upgrades.

Highlighting product reviews from experts.

Offering tips for product personalization.

Sharing community stories.

Highlighting product performance metrics.

Showcasing industry collaborations.

Explaining your product's unique selling points.

Sharing user-generated product modifications.

Demonstrating product customization options.

Highlighting your brand's sustainability efforts.

Offering exclusive promotions for followers.

Sharing your product's story.

Demonstrating the product creation process.

Offering styling tips with your product.

Highlighting user-generated how-tos.

Sharing product-related success stories.

Demonstrating product reliability.

Explaining the science behind your product.

Sharing fun facts about your product.

Highlighting customer favorites.

Demonstrating the product's practical uses.

Sharing product-related challenges.

Explaining product specifications.

Highlighting customer feedback.

Demonstrating innovative uses for your product.

Offering limited-time offers.

Sharing product care tips.

Highlighting product awards and recognitions.

Demonstrating the product's unique features.

Sharing user-generated product reviews.

Highlighting behind-the-scenes moments.

Offering exclusive discounts for TikTok followers.

Sharing product-related memes.

Highlighting your brand's community involvement.

Demonstrating product improvements.

Sharing customer journey videos.

Highlighting product-related events.

Offering tips for maximizing product use.

Demonstrating product versatility in different settings.

Sharing user-generated product hacks.

Highlighting customer transformation stories.

Explaining the inspiration behind your brand.

Sharing product-related fun facts.

Demonstrating the product's practical applications.

Highlighting user-generated content from events.

Offering exclusive promotions for TikTok followers.

Sharing product-themed trivia.

Demonstrating product reliability and durability.

Highlighting unique product features and benefits.

Sharing user-generated success stories.

Demonstrating innovative uses for your product.

Offering limited-time discounts for TikTok followers.

Sharing product-related tips and tricks.

Highlighting product awards and recognitions.

Demonstrating the product's practical uses.

Sharing user-generated content from customers.

Highlighting behind-the-scenes moments from your
brand.

Offering exclusive discounts for TikTok followers.

Sharing product-related memes and fun facts.

Highlighting your brand's community involvement and
impact.

Demonstrating product improvements and upgrades.

Sharing customer journey videos and testimonials.

Highlighting product-related events and milestones.

Offering tips for maximizing product use and benefits.

Demonstrating product versatility in different settings
and scenarios.

Sharing user-generated product hacks and tips.

Highlighting customer transformation stories and ex
periences.

Explaining the inspiration behind your brand and prod
ucts.

Sharing product-related fun facts and trivia.

Demonstrating the product's practical applications and
benefits.

Highlighting user-generated content from events and promotions.

Offering exclusive promotions and discounts for TikTok followers.

Sharing product-themed trivia and fun facts.

Demonstrating product reliability and durability in various conditions.

Highlighting unique product features and benefits.

Sharing user-generated success stories and testimonials.

Demonstrating innovative uses for your product in different scenarios.

Offering limited-time discounts and promotions for TikTok followers.

Sharing product-related tips, tricks, and hacks.

Highlighting product awards, recognitions, and achievements.

Demonstrating the product's practical uses and applications.

Sharing user-generated content from satisfied customers.

Highlighting behind-the-scenes moments from your brand and team.

Offering exclusive discounts and promotions for TikTok followers.

Sharing product-related memes, fun facts, and trivia.

Highlighting your brand's community involvement and impact.

Demonstrating product improvements, upgrades, and innovations.

Sharing customer journey videos, stories, and testimonials.

Highlighting product-related events, milestones, and achievements.

Offering tips for maximizing product use, benefits, and features.

Demonstrating product versatility in different settings, scenarios, and conditions.

Sharing user-generated product hacks, tips, and tricks.

Highlighting customer transformation stories, experiences, and testimonials.

Explaining the inspiration behind your brand, products, and mission.

Sharing product-related fun facts, trivia, and interesting information.

Demonstrating the product's practical applications,

uses, and benefits.

Highlighting user-generated content from events, promotions, and campaigns.

Offering exclusive promotions, discounts, and offers for TikTok followers.

Sharing product-themed trivia, fun facts, and interesting tidbits.

Demonstrating product reliability, durability, and performance in various conditions.

Highlighting unique product features, benefits, and selling points.

# FUN VIDEO IDEAS

Social media, as I've already mentioned, should have a big stress on the first word - SOCIAL media. It shouldn't be all sell, sell, sell. No one wants to look at pictures and videos of products without a human angle to it all.

Therefore, it's important to have fun with it as well. The videos that tend to go viral have a fun element, and could involve you, your team, or your customers, or even random people on the street (with their permission!)

Intersperse your usual content with a bit of fun and you'll soon see that your followers are engaging with you in a totally new way. Rather than putting them up randomly, you could fix a day of the week (Friday?) for always putting up a fun video, thereby providing consistency for your audience.

Here are 200 fun video ideas that could be made and put on TikTok:

Lip-sync to a popular song.

Recreate a famous movie scene.

Participate in a trending dance challenge.

Show a day in your life.

Try a viral recipe.

Share a funny pet moment.

Do a transformation video (makeup, hair, outfit).

Film a prank on a friend or family member.

Create a stop-motion animation.

Give a room tour.

Share a fun fact about yourself.

Demonstrate a unique skill or talent.

Try out a new hobby and document the process.

Do a "Get Ready With Me" (GRWM) video.

Share your favorite TikTok hacks.

Recreate a childhood photo or memory.

Show your workout routine.

Share a motivational or inspirational quote.

Play a popular TikTok game or challenge.

Create a parody of a popular trend.

Do a Q&A session.

Share your morning or night routine.

Try a viral TikTok product and review it.

Film a behind-the-scenes of your creative process.

Do a "What's in My Bag?" video.

Share your travel adventures.

Teach a new dance move.

Show a funny outtake or blooper reel.

Try a DIY project.

Do a duet with another TikToker.

Share a life hack.

Create a reaction video.

Film a slow-motion video.

Do an ASMR video.

Share your favorite memes.

Create a mashup of different TikTok trends.

Share your favorite quotes from movies or books.

Show a quick and easy recipe.

Do a "Then vs. Now" comparison.

Create a character skit.

Try on different outfits for different occasions.

Share a hidden talent.

Film a time-lapse of something creative (painting, drawing).

Do a "How To" tutorial.

Share your favorite apps or websites.

Show your pet's morning or night routine.

Create a music mashup.

Share a personal story.

Do a cooking or baking challenge.

Create a mini vlog.

Share your favorite workout moves.

Do a "Guess the Song" challenge.

Try a new beauty trend.

Share your favorite books or movies.

Film a day in the life of your pet.

Create a travel montage.

Show your skincare routine.

Do a "Draw My Life" video.

Share a funny or embarrassing story.

Film a prank call.

Create a "Types of People" video.

Do a "What I Eat in a Day" video.

Share a workout challenge.

Show a room makeover.

Do a "Guess the Emoji" challenge.

Share your favorite life hacks.

Film a day in the life at work or school.

Do a karaoke session.

Create a parody of a famous commercial.

Share your travel bucket list.

Do a blindfolded makeup challenge.

Show your favorite travel destinations.

Create a "POV" (point of view) video.

Share a throwback moment.

Film a sibling or friend tag.

Try a new sport or activity.

Do a "One Second a Day" video.

Share your favorite fashion tips.

Film a day in the life of a plant parent.

Do a "Whisper Challenge".

Share a fun science experiment.

Film a day in the life of a student.

Try a new hair color or style.

Share your favorite music playlists.

Film a day in the life of a freelancer.

Do a "Two Truths and a Lie" challenge.

Share your favorite outdoor activities.

Film a day in the life of a gamer.

Do a "Guess the Movie" challenge.

Share your favorite hobbies.

Film a day in the life of a parent.

Try a new cultural cuisine.

Share your favorite board games.

Film a day in the life of an artist.

Do a "Would You Rather" challenge.

Share your favorite holiday traditions.

Film a day in the life of a musician.

Try a new exercise routine.

Share your favorite DIY crafts.

Film a day in the life of a teacher.

Do a "Guess the Accent" challenge.

Share your favorite podcasts.

Film a day in the life of a writer.

Try a new dance style.

Share your favorite childhood memories.

Film a day in the life of a pet owner.

Do a "Guess the Flavor" challenge.

Share your favorite travel tips.

Film a day in the life of a chef.

Try a new beauty routine.

Share your favorite outdoor adventures.

Film a day in the life of a vlogger.

Do a "Try Not to Laugh" challenge.

Share your favorite tech gadgets.

Film a day in the life of a fashion designer.

Try a new cooking technique.

Share your favorite travel hacks.

Film a day in the life of a fitness instructor.

Do a "Guess the Sound" challenge.

Share your favorite productivity tips.

Film a day in the life of a photographer.

Try a new meditation or relaxation technique.

Share your favorite pet care tips.

Film a day in the life of a dancer.

Do a "Guess the Smell" challenge.

Share your favorite self-care tips.

Film a day in the life of a gardener.

Try a new art technique.

Share your favorite fashion trends.

Film a day in the life of a student athlete.

Do a "Guess the Movie Quote" challenge.

Share your favorite home decor tips.

Film a day in the life of a journalist.

Try a new skincare product.

Share your favorite music genres.

Film a day in the life of a social media manager.

Do a "Guess the Celebrity Voice" challenge.

Share your favorite writing tips.

Film a day in the life of a makeup artist.

Try a new fitness routine.

Share your favorite family traditions.

Film a day in the life of a traveler.

Do a "Guess the Emoji Combination" challenge.

Share your favorite language learning tips.

Film a day in the life of a content creator.

Try a new tech gadget.

Share your favorite video game tips.

Film a day in the life of a musician.

Do a "Guess the Song from the Lyrics" challenge.

Share your favorite study tips.

Film a day in the life of a chef.

Try a new recipe from a different culture.

Share your favorite mindfulness practices.

Film a day in the life of a fashion model.

Do a "Guess the Cartoon Character" challenge.

Share your favorite travel destinations.

Film a day in the life of a fitness trainer.

Try a new workout challenge.

Share your favorite eco-friendly tips.

Film a day in the life of a blogger.

Do a "Guess the TV Show" challenge.

Share your favorite productivity hacks.

Film a day in the life of a photographer.

Try a new creative hobby.

Share your favorite budget-friendly tips.

Film a day in the life of a painter.

Do a "Guess the Historical Figure" challenge.

Share your favorite inspirational quotes.

Film a day in the life of a dancer.

Try a new dance routine.

Share your favorite motivational tips.

Film a day in the life of a student.

Do a "Guess the Country" challenge.

Share your favorite relaxation techniques.

Film a day in the life of a writer.

Try a new writing prompt.

Share your favorite book recommendations.

Film a day in the life of a teacher.

Do a "Guess the Language" challenge.

Share your favorite educational resources.

Film a day in the life of a gardener.

Try a new gardening technique.

Share your favorite sustainability tips.

Film a day in the life of a makeup artist.

Do a "Guess the Makeup Product" challenge.

Share your favorite beauty tips.

Film a day in the life of a vlogger.

Try a new filming technique.

Share your favorite video editing tips.

Film a day in the life of a content creator.

Do a "Guess the Movie Plot" challenge.

Share your favorite filmmaking tips.

Film a day in the life of a social media influencer.

Try a new social media strategy.

Share your favorite branding tips.

Film a day in the life of a business owner.

Do a "Guess the Company Logo" challenge.

Share your favorite entrepreneurial tips.

Film a day in the life of a marketer.

Try a new marketing technique and share how it goes with your followers (the zanier the idea, the better).

# INFLUENCER VIDEO IDEAS

Maybe you're shy. Maybe your team are fed up with being on camera. Maybe you've got a few hot new influencers, who've slid into your DM's asking you if they can work with you.

Whatever the reason, getting influencers and brand partners to create videos of themselves using or talking about your product can be a quick way to success. We've all seen Kim Kardashian promoting products that have then sold out, and in some cases that popularity has kept the brand afloat for years.

Influencers aren't going anywhere, and should be considered (budget dependent) when putting together your TikTok strategy. Not only can you post the video on your own account, but you can also ask them to post it on theirs, getting maximum visibility.

Here are 100 video ideas for involving influencers or brand partners:

Unboxing Collaboration: Unbox products sent by a partner brand.

Day in the Life: Show a day in the life using a partner's product.

Product Review: Give an honest review of a partner's product.

Giveaway Announcement: Announce a joint giveaway with a partner brand.

Tutorial: Teach viewers how to use a partner's product.

Q&A Session: Answer questions about the partnered product.

Behind-the-Scenes: Show behind-the-scenes footage of a collaboration.

Duet Challenge: Do a duet challenge with another influencer.

Transformation Video: Use a partner's product for a makeover.

How It's Made: Visit a partner's factory or office.

Taste Test: Try a partner's food or drink products.

Live Stream: Host a live stream with a partner brand.

Trending Challenge: Participate in a trending TikTok challenge with a partner's product.

Pack With Me: Pack for a trip using items from a partner brand.

Unboxing Reaction: Film your genuine reaction to unboxing a partner's product.

Product Comparison: Compare a partner's product with others in the market.

Storytime: Share a personal story involving a partner's product.

Mystery Box: Open a mystery box from a partner brand.

DIY Project: Create a DIY project using a partner's product.

Fitness Challenge: Try a fitness challenge using a partner's equipment.

Before and After: Show before and after results using a partner's product.

Fashion Haul: Showcase a clothing haul from a partner brand.

Recipe Video: Make a recipe using ingredients from a partner brand.

Dance Collaboration: Perform a dance routine with another influencer.

Holiday Special: Create holiday-themed content with a partner brand.

Event Coverage: Cover a partner's event or launch.

Travel Vlog: Feature a partner's travel accessories in a vlog.

Pet Video: Showcase a pet using a partner's product.

Fan Shoutouts: Give shoutouts to fans using a partner's product.

Product Hints: Give hints about a new product launch from a partner.

Room Makeover: Do a room makeover using a partner's decor items.

Educational Content: Educate viewers on how a partner's product works.

Top 5 Tips: Share top tips using a partner's product.

Collaborative Giveaways: Partner with other influencers for a giveaway.

Reaction Video: React to a partner's advert or campaign.

Flash Sale Announcement: Announce a partner's flash sale.

Shopping Spree: Go on a shopping spree at a partner's store.

Product Testing: Test a partner's product live.

Cooking Show: Host a mini cooking show with a partner's ingredients.

Makeup Tutorial: Create a makeup look using a partner's cosmetics.

Travel Essentials: Show travel essentials from a partner brand.

Birthday Special: Celebrate your birthday with a partner's product.

Fitness Routine: Share your fitness routine featuring a partner's gear.

Tech Review: Review a gadget from a partner brand.

Festival Prep: Prepare for a festival using items from a partner.

Sleep Routine: Show your sleep routine using a partner's products.

Holiday Packing: Pack for a holiday with essentials from a partner.

Product Launch: Announce a partner's new product launch.

Morning Routine: Share your morning routine featuring a partner's product.

Fan Interaction: Interact with fans using a partner's product.

Challenge a Friend: Challenge a friend to use a partner's product.

Seasonal Trends: Highlight seasonal trends with a partner's products.

Game Night: Host a game night using a partner's games.

Charity Collaboration: Partner with a brand for a charity event.

Favourite Products: Showcase your favourite products from a partner.

Eco-Friendly Tips: Share eco-friendly tips using a partner's products.

Spa Day: Have a spa day at home with a partner's products.

Book Club: Start a book club with books from a partner.

Craft Time: Do a crafting session using a partner's supplies.

Pet Adoption: Feature a pet adoption event with a partner.

Career Advice: Share career advice with a partner's tools.

Fashion Show: Host a mini fashion show with a partner's clothing line.

Garden Tips: Share gardening tips using a partner's products.

Music Video: Create a music video featuring a partner's products.

Health Tips: Share health tips using a partner's wellness products.

Room Tour: Give a room tour featuring a partner's decor.

Surprise Unboxing: Unbox a surprise package from a partner.

Bucket List: Create a bucket list using a partner's experiences.

DIY Skincare: Make DIY skincare products with a partner's ingredients.

Fan Meet-Up: Host a fan meet-up featuring a partner's products.

Outdoor Adventure: Go on an outdoor adventure with a partner's gear.

Summer Essentials: Share summer essentials from a partner.

Favourite Recipes: Share your favourite recipes using a partner's ingredients.

Winter Warmers: Highlight winter warmers from a

partner.

Home Workout: Share a home workout using a partner's equipment.

Holiday Gift Guide: Create a holiday gift guide with a partner's products.

Book Review: Review a book from a partner's collection.

Camping Trip: Plan a camping trip with a partner's gear.

Festival Look: Create a festival look with a partner's products.

Wardrobe Essentials: Share wardrobe essentials from a partner.

First Impressions: Give first impressions of a partner's new product.

Monthly Favourites: Share your monthly favourites from a partner.

Seasonal Decor: Showcase seasonal decor from a partner.

Virtual Event: Host a virtual event with a partner brand.

Self-Care Day: Have a self-care day with a partner's products.

Eco-Friendly Haul: Do an eco-friendly haul with a partner's products.

Date Night: Plan a date night featuring a partner's products.

Home Renovation: Show a home renovation using a partner's products.

Fitness Gear Review: Review fitness gear from a partner.

Tech Tutorial: Create a tech tutorial using a partner's gadget.

Collaborative Playlist: Create a collaborative playlist with a partner.

Snack Review: Review snacks from a partner brand.

Fashion Tips: Share fashion tips using a partner's clothing line.

Seasonal Outfit: Showcase a seasonal outfit from a partner.

Live Q&A: Host a live Q&A with a partner brand

representative.

Home Office Tour: Give a tour of your home office featuring a partner's products.

Creative Writing Tips: Share creative writing tips using a partner's tools.

Eco-Friendly DIY: Do an eco-friendly DIY project with a partner's products.

Collaboration Announcement: Announce a new collaboration with a partner.

Seasonal Recipes: Share seasonal recipes using a partner's ingredients or as a co-production.

# COMPANY VISION VIDEO IDEAS

Here are 100 TikTok video ideas to share your company vision:

Introduction to Your Company Vision: Briefly explain your company's vision.

Founder's Story: Share how the founder's vision inspired the company.

Mission Statement: Explain your mission statement and what it means to your company.

Vision in Action: Show examples of your vision being implemented in everyday business.

Employee Stories: Feature employees sharing how they contribute to the company vision.

Customer Testimonials: Share customer stories that align with your company's vision.

Company Values: Discuss the core values that drive your vision.

Sustainability Efforts: Highlight how your company is working towards a sustainable future.

Community Involvement: Showcase your company's involvement in local communities.

Innovation: Share how your company is innovating to achieve its vision.

Behind the Scenes: Give a behind-the-scenes look at your daily operations.

Diversity and Inclusion: Highlight your efforts towards creating a diverse and inclusive workplace.

Future Goals: Discuss your company's future goals and how they align with your vision.

Employee Spotlight: Feature employees who embody the company vision.

Success Stories: Share success stories that reflect your company's vision.

Company Culture: Show what it's like to work at your company.

Vision-Driven Projects: Highlight specific projects that are driven by your vision.

Product Development: Explain how your products align with your company vision.

Leadership Message: Share a message from the leadership team about the company vision.

Customer Impact: Show how your products or services positively impact customers.

Ethical Practices: Discuss your company's ethical practices and how they align with your vision.

Innovation Lab: Give a tour of your innovation lab or R&D department.

Training Programs: Highlight training programs that align with your company's vision.

Employee Development: Show how you invest in employee development.

Corporate Social Responsibility: Explain your corporate social responsibility initiatives.

Partnerships: Highlight partnerships that support

your vision.

Volunteer Work: Showcase your company's volunteer efforts.

Company Milestones: Celebrate company milestones that reflect your vision.

Customer Feedback: Share customer feedback that supports your vision.

Vision Board: Create a vision board video for your company's future.

Green Initiatives: Highlight your company's green initiatives.

Inclusive Hiring: Discuss your inclusive hiring practices.

Employee Benefits: Explain how your employee benefits support your vision.

Vision for Growth: Talk about your vision for the company's growth.

Sustainable Products: Showcase products that are sustainable or eco-friendly.

Work-Life Balance: Show how your company promotes work-life balance.

Health and Wellness: Highlight your health and wellness programs.

Mentorship Programs: Feature your mentorship programs.

Product Impact: Show how your products make a difference in the world.

Visionary Leadership: Discuss the role of visionary leadership in your company.

Office Tour: Give a tour of your office, highlighting spaces that support your vision.

Annual Reports: Summarise key points from your annual reports that align with your vision.

Career Growth: Share stories of career growth within your company.

Sustainable Sourcing: Discuss your efforts towards sustainable sourcing.

Innovation Challenges: Highlight any innovation challenges or hackathons you host.

Customer-Centric Approach: Show how you put customers at the centre of your vision.

Team Building: Showcase team-building activities.

Global Reach: Discuss your company's global reach and impact.

Cultural Events: Highlight cultural events that support your vision.

Learning and Development: Showcase learning and development opportunities.

Employee Testimonials: Share testimonials from employees about the company vision.

Vision in Marketing: Explain how your marketing strategy aligns with your vision.

Product Lifecycle: Show the lifecycle of your products.

Workshops and Seminars: Highlight workshops and seminars that support your vision.

Customer Success Stories: Share stories of customer success.

Collaborative Projects: Showcase collaborative projects with other companies.

Visionary Quotes: Share quotes from company leaders about the vision.

Supplier Partnerships: Highlight partnerships with ethical suppliers.

Visionary Innovations: Discuss visionary innovations within your company.

Awards and Recognitions: Showcase awards and recognitions that align with your vision.

Visionary Technologies: Highlight the technologies driving your vision.

Community Impact: Show how your company impacts the community positively.

Visionary Campaigns: Share marketing campaigns that reflect your vision.

Eco-Friendly Office: Show how your office is eco-friendly.

Leadership Insights: Share insights from your leadership team.

Product Launches: Highlight new product launches.

Visionary Partnerships: Discuss strategic partnerships that support your vision.

Corporate Values: Explain your corporate values and

how they drive your vision.

Sustainable Practices: Highlight sustainable practices within your company.

Employee Engagement: Show how you engage employees in your vision.

Innovation Hub: Give a tour of your innovation hub.

Customer Loyalty: Discuss customer loyalty and its importance to your vision.

Company Retreats: Highlight company retreats and their purpose.

Employee Wellness: Show how you support employee wellness.

Visionary Products: Showcase products that embody your vision.

Leadership Q&A: Host a Q&A with your leadership team.

Community Projects: Highlight community projects you're involved in.

Visionary Strategies: Discuss strategies that support your vision.

Company History: Share the history of your company and its vision.

Visionary Quotes: Share inspiring quotes that reflect your vision.

Sustainability Goals: Discuss your sustainability goals.

Employee Programs: Highlight programs that support employee development.

Customer Impact: Show how your company impacts customers positively.

Visionary Goals: Share your company's visionary goals.

Product Innovation: Discuss product innovations.

Visionary Leadership: Highlight leadership that drives your vision.

Sustainable Office: Show how your office is sustainable.

Customer Engagement: Discuss customer engagement strategies.

Employee Stories: Share stories of employees who embody the company vision.

Community Impact: Show the impact of your company on the community.

Visionary Projects: Highlight projects that reflect your vision.

Product Impact: Show the impact of your products.

Corporate Responsibility: Discuss your corporate responsibility initiatives.

Employee Growth: Share stories of employee growth.

Innovation Journey: Discuss your innovation journey.

Visionary Campaigns: Share campaigns that reflect your vision.

Company Culture: Highlight aspects of your company culture.

Sustainable Initiatives: Showcase your sustainable initiatives.

Leadership Vision: Share the leadership vision for the company.

Visionary Events: Highlight events that support

your vision.

These ideas should help you create engaging TikTok content that effectively communicates your company's vision.

# BUSINESS ADVICE TIKTOK VIDEOS

People want entertainment, but they also want wisdom. There are millions of posts for quote of the day, and general business advice. As an entrepreneur, or someone who's hands on in the day-to-day running of the business, you have heaps of advice that you might not even know about.

People want to hear that advice.

Here are 100 TikTok video ideas for sharing business advice:

Introductory Business Tips: Share basic business advice for beginners.

Starting a Business: Steps to start a new business.

Writing a Business Plan: Key elements of a solid business plan.

Market Research Tips: How to conduct effective market research.

Finding Your Niche: Tips for identifying your business niche.

Setting Business Goals: How to set and achieve business goals.

Business Financing: Options for financing your business.

Budgeting for Small Businesses: Budgeting tips for new businesses.

Creating a Brand: Steps to create a strong brand identity.

Marketing Strategies: Effective marketing strategies for small businesses.

Social Media Marketing: Tips for using social media to promote your business.

SEO Basics: Basic SEO tips for business websites.

Content Marketing: How to create engaging content for your audience.

Email Marketing: Building an effective email marketing campaign.

Networking Tips: How to network effectively in your industry.

Customer Service: Importance of excellent customer service.

Time Management: Tips for managing your time effectively as a business owner.

Productivity Hacks: Simple productivity hacks for busy entrepreneurs.

Work-Life Balance: How to maintain work-life balance as a business owner.

Leadership Skills: Essential leadership skills for business success.

Delegating Tasks: How to delegate tasks effectively.

Building a Team: Tips for building a strong business team.

Hiring Employees: Key considerations when hiring your first employees.

Employee Training: Importance of training and

development.

Managing Finances: Financial management tips for small businesses.

Cash Flow Management: How to manage your cash flow effectively.

Pricing Strategies: Setting the right prices for your products or services.

Customer Retention: Strategies for retaining your customers.

Sales Techniques: Effective sales techniques for business growth.

Pitching to Investors: How to pitch your business to potential investors.

Business Analytics: Using data to drive business decisions.

Risk Management: Identifying and managing business risks.

Legal Advice: Common legal considerations for small businesses.

Trademarking Your Brand: How to trademark your business name or logo.

Building a Website: Tips for creating an effective business website.

E-commerce Tips: How to start and grow an online store.

Product Development: Steps to develop new products.

Business Scaling: How to scale your business effectively.

Customer Feedback: Using customer feedback to improve your business.

Building Business Relationships: Importance of building strong business relationships.

Negotiation Tips: Effective negotiation techniques.

Adapting to Change: How to adapt to changes in the market.

Crisis Management: Tips for managing a business crisis.

Sustainability in Business: How to make your business more sustainable.

Technology in Business: Leveraging technology to

improve business operations.

Productivity Tools: Recommended productivity tools for business owners.

Goal Setting: How to set and achieve business goals.

Business Trends: Current trends in your industry.

Remote Working: Tips for managing a remote team.

Project Management: Basics of effective project management.

Customer Acquisition: Strategies for acquiring new customers.

Marketing on a Budget: Low-cost marketing strategies.

Building a Community: How to build a community around your brand.

Event Marketing: Tips for promoting and hosting business events.

Public Relations: Importance of PR and how to get started.

Digital Marketing: Key digital marketing strategies.

Collaborations and Partnerships: How to collaborate with other businesses.

Product Launches: Tips for a successful product launch.

Competitor Analysis: How to analyse your competitors.

Business Ethics: Importance of ethics in business.

Creating Business Systems: Setting up systems for efficiency.

Innovative Thinking: Encouraging innovation within your business.

Customer Personas: Creating and using customer personas.

Brand Storytelling: How to tell your brand's story effectively.

Using Analytics: Leveraging analytics for business growth.

Funding Options: Different funding options for startups.

Writing Proposals: How to write effective business proposals.

Business Taxes: Basic tax tips for business owners.

Financial Forecasting: How to forecast your business finances.

Building Credibility: Ways to build credibility and trust.

Business Adaptability: Adapting your business to market changes.

Healthy Work Environment: Creating a positive work environment.

Personal Development: Importance of personal development for business success.

Industry Networking: How to network within your industry.

Developing a USP: Creating a unique selling proposition.

Effective Meetings: Tips for running effective business meetings.

Business Journals: Keeping a business journal for tracking progress.

Seasonal Marketing: Planning seasonal marketing

campaigns.

Building a Brand Identity: How to build a strong brand identity.

Influencer Marketing: Using influencers to promote your business.

Maintaining Momentum: Keeping your business momentum going.

Customer Loyalty Programmes: Setting up customer loyalty programmes.

Franchising Your Business: Basics of franchising your business.

Disaster Recovery: Planning for disaster recovery in business.

Exit Strategy: Developing an exit strategy for your business.

Time Blocking: Using time blocking to increase productivity.

Mindset for Success: Developing a success-oriented mindset.

Finding Mentors: How to find and work with business mentors.

Crowdfunding Tips: Tips for a successful crowdfunding campaign.

Public Speaking: Importance of public speaking skills for business.

Creating a Vision Statement: How to create a powerful vision statement.

Adapting Marketing Strategies: Adapting marketing strategies over time.

Content Creation: Creating engaging content for your audience.

Managing Business Growth: Managing growth effectively.

Building an Online Presence: Building a strong online presence.

Effective Advertising: Tips for creating effective advertisements.

Startup Mistakes: Common startup mistakes and how to avoid them.

Productivity Apps: Recommended apps for business productivity.

Customer Journey Mapping: Mapping out the customer journey.

Setting KPIs: Setting and tracking key performance indicators.


These ideas should provide a comprehensive range of topics to help you share valuable business advice on TikTok.

# LIFEHACKS VIDEO IDEAS

What else do people want to see? What else goes viral, and helps people out?

Life hacks, of course! If you don't believe me, just look up #lifehack on TikTok. You'll soon come running back, tail between your legs.

It might be time for me to point out something very important. You shouldn't deviate too wildly from your business when making these videos (not just life hacks, but any of them).

If you run a dog grooming business, then a life hack for washing your car might not be that interesting to your dog-loving followers. If you've set up your own legal firm specialising in divorces, then your 'How to peel an orange' video might go viral, but probably won't lead to that many enquiries.

Try and make all of your videos at least somewhat relevant for your niche and your audience.

If you <u>are</u> a divorce lawyer and you've hit a couple of life hack viral videos, then please do get in touch and let me know what they were all about. While peeling an orange might be one way to keep a spouse, I'm intrigued about the other fun hacks you might have come up with.

Anyway, without further rambling, here are 100 TikTok video ideas for sharing life hacks:

Organising Your Closet: Tips for a clutter-free wardrobe.

Time Management: Simple tricks to manage your time better.

Meal Prepping: Easy meal prep ideas for the week.

DIY Cleaning Solutions: Making eco-friendly cleaning products.

Budgeting Tips: How to create and stick to a budget.

Travel Packing: Efficient packing hacks for travel.

Quick Breakfast Ideas: Fast and healthy breakfast recipes.

Tech Shortcuts: Useful shortcuts for your smartphone.

Study Tips: Effective study hacks for students.

Healthy Snacks: Easy and nutritious snack ideas.

Home Workout: Quick exercises you can do at home.

Car Maintenance: Simple car maintenance tips.

Productivity Hacks: Boost your productivity with these tips.

Laundry Tips: Tricks to make laundry easier.

Household Organisation: Organising your home efficiently.

Stress Relief: Simple techniques to reduce stress.

Grocery Shopping: Tips to save money on groceries.

Skin Care: DIY skincare routines and tips.

Gardening Tips: Easy gardening hacks for beginners.

Pet Care: Useful hacks for pet owners.

Home Decor: Affordable home decorating ideas.

Fitness Tips: Easy ways to stay fit and healthy.

Saving Money: Creative ways to save money daily.

DIY Repairs: Simple home repair hacks.

Hair Care: Quick and easy hair care tips.

Travel Hacks: Tips for smoother and cheaper travel.

Cooking Tips: Time-saving cooking techniques.

Work-Life Balance: Tips for maintaining work-life balance.

Eco-Friendly Living: Easy ways to live more sustainably.

Study Habits: Hacks to improve your study habits.

Public Speaking: Tips to improve public speaking skills.

Office Organisation: Keeping your workspace organised.

Diet Tips: Simple tips to improve your diet.

Home Security: Affordable home security hacks.

Morning Routine: Creating an effective morning routine.

Baking Tips: Easy baking hacks for beginners.

Language Learning: Tips for learning a new language.

DIY Projects: Fun and easy DIY project ideas.

Self-Care: Simple self-care tips for a better you.

Fashion Hacks: Quick fashion fixes and tips.

Reducing Waste: Tips to reduce waste in your home.

Mindfulness: Practicing mindfulness in everyday life.

Healthy Habits: Building and maintaining healthy habits.

Motivation Tips: Staying motivated and productive.

Cooking on a Budget: Delicious meals on a tight budget.

Cleaning Tips: Quick and effective cleaning hacks.

Pet Training: Easy training tips for pets.

Social Media Tips: Growing your social media presence.

Job Interview Tips: Preparing for job interviews.

Personal Finance: Managing your personal finances.

Stress-Free Travel: Making travel stress-free.

Sleep Tips: Improving your sleep quality.

Healthy Lifestyle: Tips for a healthier lifestyle.

Quick Fixes: Simple solutions for everyday problems.

DIY Crafts: Fun and easy craft ideas.

Pet Nutrition: Tips for feeding your pets.

Home Improvement: Affordable home improvement tips.

Cleaning Gadgets: Using gadgets to clean efficiently.

Work-from-Home Tips: Maximising productivity at home.

Language Tips: Improving your language skills.

Energy Saving: Saving energy at home.

Healthy Recipes: Quick and healthy recipe ideas.

Decluttering Tips: Decluttering your home efficiently.

Diet Hacks: Simple hacks to improve your diet.

Public Speaking: Overcoming fear of public speaking.

Mental Health Tips: Taking care of your mental health.

Pet Grooming: Easy pet grooming hacks.

Organising Paperwork: Keeping your paperwork organised.

Quick Meals: Preparing quick and easy meals.

Stress-Free Mornings: Making your mornings stress-free.

Baking Shortcuts: Easy shortcuts for baking.

Gardening on a Budget: Affordable gardening tips.

Smart Shopping: Getting the best deals while shopping.

Self-Improvement: Tips for personal development.

Fitness Motivation: Staying motivated to work out.

Healthy Mindset: Developing a healthy mindset.

Car Cleaning: Tips for keeping your car clean.

Efficient Studying: Studying more effectively.

Daily Routine: Creating a productive daily routine.

Eco-Friendly Tips: Living more eco-friendly.

Pet Safety: Keeping your pets safe at home.

Creative Hobbies: Finding and enjoying creative hobbies.

Budget Travel: Tips for travelling on a budget.

Office Hacks: Making your office life easier.

Diet Planning: Planning your diet effectively.

Digital Organisation: Keeping your digital life organised.

Stress-Free Work: Reducing stress at work.

Home Storage: Maximising storage space at home.

Health Tips: Simple tips for better health.

Productivity Tools: Using tools to boost productivity.

Morning Hacks: Making your mornings more efficient.

Healthy Eating: Tips for healthier eating habits.

Pet Travel: Tips for travelling with pets.

Sustainable Living: Living more sustainably.

Study Techniques: Effective study techniques.

Time-Saving Tips: Saving time in your daily routine.

Financial Tips: Managing your finances better.

Home Hacks: Simple hacks for a better home.

Daily Hacks: Everyday hacks to make life easier.

Personal Growth: Tips for personal growth and improvement.

These ideas should provide a wide range of useful and engaging content for your TikTok audience.

# HOW TO HAVE BANTER

Captions play a crucial role in enhancing the impact of your TikTok videos. A well-crafted caption can grab attention, provoke thought, and encourage interaction. This chapter will guide you through the art of writing witty and engaging captions that resonate with your audience and boost your TikTok presence.

1. Understanding Your Audience

Before you start writing captions, it's important to understand who your audience is. Consider their age, interests, sense of humour, and what kind of content they enjoy. Tailoring your captions to your audience's preferences can make them more relatable and engaging.

## 2. Keep It Short and Sweet

TikTok is all about quick, bite-sized content, and your captions should reflect that. Aim for brevity while still conveying your message. Short, punchy captions are more likely to catch your audience's eye and keep their attention.

Example: Instead of "This is a tutorial on how to make a delicious smoothie," try "Smoothie magic in 30 seconds!"

## 3. Use Emojis Wisely

Emojis can add a fun and visual element to your captions. They help convey emotions and break up text, making your caption more visually appealing. However, use them sparingly to avoid clutter.

Example: "Feeling those Monday blues? ☕ #CoffeeLovers"

## 4. Incorporate Humour

Witty and humorous captions can make your content more memorable. Play with puns, wordplay, and light-hearted jokes that align with your brand's voice and the video's content.

Example: For a video of a cat knocking over a plant,

you might write, "Plants? Not on my watch. 🌿🐾 #CatLife"

## 5. Ask Questions

Engage your audience by asking questions. This encourages viewers to comment and interact with your video, boosting engagement and visibility.

Example: "Pineapple on pizza: love it or hate it? 🍍🍕 #Debate"

## 6. Use Hashtags Strategically

Hashtags can increase your video's discoverability. Use a mix of popular and niche hashtags relevant to your content. Avoid overloading your caption with too many hashtags; 3-5 well-chosen ones are usually enough.

Example: "Weekend DIY project! 🔨 #DIY #HomeDecor #WeekendVibes"

## 7. Include a Call to Action

Encourage viewers to take action by including a call to action (CTA) in your captions. This could be as simple as asking them to like, comment, share, or follow.

Example: "Enjoyed this recipe? Tap the heart and

follow for more! ❤️ #CookingTips"

8. Tell a Story

Briefly tell a story or share a personal anecdote that relates to your video. This can make your content more relatable and engaging.

Example: "This cake recipe has been in my family for generations! #FamilyRecipes"

9. Stay Relevant with Trends

Incorporate current trends, slang, and popular culture references in your captions to stay relevant and connect with a broader audience.

Example: "Just trying to keep up with the Gen Z dance moves! #DanceChallenge #GenZ"

10. Showcase Your Personality

Let your personality shine through your captions. Whether you're quirky, serious, or laid-back, authentic captions can help build a stronger connection with your audience.

Example: "Attempting yoga... but my dog had other plans. #PetYoga"

11. Utilise Engagement Hooks

Start your captions with engagement hooks to draw in your audience. Phrases like "Wait for it," "You won't believe this," or "Guess what happens next" can pique curiosity and encourage viewers to watch till the end.

Example: "Wait for it... the surprise twist at the end is worth it! #Unexpected"

## 12. Match the Tone of Your Video

Ensure that your caption complements the tone of your video. A funny video should have a humorous caption, while a serious or emotional video might have a more heartfelt message.

Example: For a motivational video, write, "Believe in yourself – every step counts. #MotivationMonday"

## 13. Highlight the Value

Emphasise the value viewers will get from watching your video. Whether it's a life hack, a tip, or just a good laugh, make it clear what they can expect.

Example: "Learn how to fold a fitted sheet like a pro! #LifeHacks"

## 14. Experiment and Analyse

Experiment with different types of captions to see what resonates most with your audience. Analyse your engagement metrics to understand which captions perform best and adjust your strategy accordingly.

Example: Try varying your approach – one video might have a humorous caption, while another might be more informative. Compare the engagement rates to see which works better.

**Conclusion**
Crafting witty and engaging captions for your TikTok videos can significantly enhance your content's appeal and boost interaction with your audience. By understanding your audience, keeping it concise, incorporating humour, asking questions, and staying relevant, you can create captions that not only complement your videos but also engage your viewers on a deeper level.

Remember, the key to great captions is to reflect your personality, provide value, and encourage interaction. With these tips and a bit of creativity, you'll be well on your way to mastering the art of TikTok captions.

Happy captioning!

# ALLOCATING SOCIAL MEDIA BUDGET

Effective budget allocation is crucial for maximizing the impact of your social media efforts. Whether you're a small business owner, a marketer, or an influencer, understanding how to distribute your social media budget can help you achieve your goals more efficiently. This chapter provides a comprehensive guide to allocating your social media budget across various activities and platforms.

**1. Understanding Your Goals**

Before you allocate your budget, it's essential to clearly define your social media goals. Common goals include:

Brand Awareness: Increasing the visibility of your brand.

Engagement: Encouraging likes, comments, shares, and interactions.

Lead Generation: Capturing potential customer information.

Sales and Conversions: Driving purchases or conversions.

Customer Support: Providing assistance and building customer relationships.

Each goal may require different strategies and budget allocations. For instance, brand awareness campaigns might focus more on reach and impressions, while lead generation efforts might invest heavily in targeted ads and content.

## 2. Breakdown of Social Media Activities

Allocating your budget effectively requires understanding the different activities involved in your social media strategy:

Content Creation: Producing high-quality content, including photos, videos, graphics, and written posts.

Advertising: Running paid campaigns on platforms like TikTok, Instagram, Facebook, and LinkedIn.

Influencer Partnerships: Collaborating with influencers to promote your brand or products.

Tools and Software: Investing in tools for scheduling, analytics, design, and video editing.

Community Management: Engaging with your audience through comments, messages, and social media groups.

Training and Development: Upskilling your team to stay current with social media trends and best practices.

## 3. Allocating Budget Across Platforms

Different platforms may require different budget allocations based on their audience, format, and engagement levels. Here's a suggested breakdown:

TikTok:

Content Creation (30%): Invest in creative, engaging videos that resonate with TikTok's audience.

Advertising (30%): Use TikTok Ads for targeted campaigns to reach a broader audience.

Influencer Partnerships (20%): Collaborate with TikTok influencers to leverage their reach and authenticity.

Tools and Software (10%): Use tools for video editing and analytics to optimize content.

Community Management (10%): Engage with your audience through comments and duets.

Instagram:

Content Creation (25%): Focus on high-quality images, stories, and IGTV videos.

Advertising (35%): Utilize Instagram Ads for promotions, especially stories and carousel ads.

Influencer Partnerships (20%): Partner with Instagram influencers for authentic promotion.

Tools and Software (10%): Invest in scheduling and analytics tools like Later or Hootsuite.

Community Management (10%): Regularly interact with followers through comments, DMs, and live sessions.

Facebook:

Content Creation (20%): Create diverse content

including posts, videos, and stories.

Advertising (40%): Leverage Facebook Ads for targeted campaigns with detailed demographics.

Influencer Partnerships (15%): Collaborate with Facebook influencers or groups.

Tools and Software (10%): Use tools for managing ads, like Facebook Ads Manager.

Community Management (15%): Engage with your audience in groups and through comments.

LinkedIn:

Content Creation (25%): Focus on professional content, articles, and thought leadership posts.

Advertising (30%): Use LinkedIn Ads for B2B lead generation and professional networking.

Influencer Partnerships (15%): Partner with industry leaders for credibility and reach.

Tools and Software (10%): Utilize analytics and scheduling tools like Buffer.

Community Management (20%): Engage in professional discussions and respond to comments and messages.

## 4. Budget Flexibility

While the above allocations provide a framework, it's essential to remain flexible. Social media trends and platform algorithms can change, requiring adjustments to your strategy and budget. Monitor the performance of your campaigns regularly and be prepared to reallocate funds based on what's working best.

## 5. Maximising ROI

To ensure you get the most out of your social media budget, consider these tips:

Track Performance: Use analytics tools to track the performance of your content and ads. This data will help you make informed decisions about where to allocate your budget.

Test and Learn: Experiment with different types of content and ad formats to see what resonates with your audience. A/B testing can be particularly useful.

Focus on High-Performing Channels: If certain platforms or types of content consistently perform well, consider allocating more budget to those areas.

Engage Your Audience: Building a loyal and engaged

audience can provide long-term benefits that go beyond immediate metrics.

## 6. Planning for the Future

As you plan your budget, keep an eye on emerging trends and technologies. Platforms like TikTok are continually evolving, and new social media channels are always on the horizon. Stay informed about the latest developments to ensure your strategy remains cutting-edge.

## Conclusion

Effective budget allocation is critical for maximizing the impact of your social media efforts. By understanding your goals, breaking down your activities, and strategically distributing your budget across platforms, you can ensure that your social media strategy is both efficient and effective. Stay flexible, track your performance, and be prepared to adapt as the social media landscape continues to evolve.

With a well-planned budget and a strategic approach, you can achieve significant success on TikTok and other social media platforms. Happy planning and executing!

# FILMING AND PHOTOGRAPHY

Creating visually appealing content is key to capturing your audience's attention on TikTok. High-quality filming and photography can significantly enhance the impact of your videos, making them more engaging and shareable. This bonus chapter will guide you through the best practices for filming and photography to help you elevate your TikTok game.

**Essential Equipment**

While TikTok's charm partly lies in its ability to showcase raw and spontaneous content, investing in a few key pieces of equipment can drastically improve your production quality.

Smartphone: Modern smartphones are equipped

with high-quality cameras that are more than sufficient for TikTok. Ensure your phone has a good camera resolution and supports 1080p video recording.

Tripod: A tripod stabilises your shots and eliminates shaky footage. Choose a flexible tripod that can be adjusted to different heights and angles.

Lighting: Good lighting is crucial. Natural light is ideal, but ring lights or softbox lights can provide consistent and flattering illumination.

Microphone: Audio quality is just as important as video quality. Consider using an external microphone to capture clear sound, especially for talking segments.

Editing Software: Invest in user-friendly editing apps like Adobe Premiere Rush, InShot, or TikTok's built-in editor to enhance your videos with effects, transitions, and music.

**Filming Techniques**

To create engaging TikTok videos, it's essential to master some basic filming techniques.

Stable Shots: Use a tripod or stabiliser to keep your shots steady. If you're filming handheld, use both hands and keep your elbows close to your body.

Framing: Follow the rule of thirds. Imagine your screen divided into nine equal parts by two horizontal and two vertical lines. Place your subject along these lines or at their intersections for a balanced composition.

Lighting: Position your primary light source in front of you to avoid harsh shadows. Natural light is best, but if indoors, use a ring light or softbox for even lighting.

Background: Ensure your background is clean and uncluttered. Use solid colours or simple patterns to avoid distracting your audience from the main subject.

Angles: Experiment with different angles to add interest. High angles can make subjects appear smaller and more vulnerable, while low angles can give a sense of power.

Movement: Use movement to create dynamic videos. Pan your camera slowly to the left or right, or move it up and down to create a sense of motion.

Transitions: Plan your transitions while filming. Quick cuts, match cuts, and seamless transitions can make your video more engaging.

**Photography Techniques**

High-quality photos can enhance your TikTok presence by serving as thumbnails or standalone posts.

Lighting: Use natural light whenever possible. Early morning and late afternoon provide the best lighting conditions, known as the golden hour.

Composition: Apply the rule of thirds, symmetry, and leading lines to create visually appealing compositions. Avoid clutter and ensure the focus is on the main subject.

Depth of Field: Use portrait mode on your smartphone to achieve a shallow depth of field, which blurs the background and highlights the subject.

Angles and Perspectives: Experiment with various angles to add creativity. Shoot from high above, ground level, or unusual perspectives to capture unique shots.

Editing: Use photo editing apps like Lightroom, Snapseed, or VSCO to enhance your photos. Adjust brightness, contrast, and saturation, and apply filters for a polished look.

**Tips for Specific Content Types**

Tutorials and How-To Videos: Use a tripod for stable shots and ensure good lighting. Film close-ups of your hands when demonstrating products or techniques.

Product Showcases: Use a clean background and good lighting. Include close-ups to highlight product details. Use slow-motion shots for added effect.

Vlogs: Combine different angles and include a mix of wide, medium, and close-up shots. Capture candid moments to add authenticity.

Dances and Challenges: Use a wide shot to capture full-body movements. Ensure the background is clear to avoid distractions.

Interviews and Q&As: Use a tripod and external microphone. Position the camera at eye level for a natural look. Ensure the background is clean and well-lit.

**Editing Tips**

Editing is where your video comes together. Here are some tips for effective editing:

Cut to the Beat: Sync your cuts and transitions with the beat of the background music to create a rhythmic and engaging video.

Use Transitions: Smooth transitions between shots keep the viewer engaged. Experiment with match cuts, jump cuts, and creative transitions available in editing apps.

Add Text and Graphics: Use text overlays and graphics to highlight key points, provide context, or add a call to action.

Keep it Short and Sweet: TikTok's format favours short, snappy content. Aim to keep your videos concise and to the point.

Colour Correction: Adjust the colours to make your video look more professional. Use filters and colour correction tools to enhance the visual appeal.

**Final Thoughts**

Mastering filming and photography for TikTok requires a blend of creativity, technical skills, and strategic planning. By investing in the right equipment, learning essential filming and photography techniques, and using effective editing practices, you can create high-quality content that stands out on TikTok. Remember, the most important aspect is to have fun and let your personality shine through. Happy filming!

# WHY NOT INSTAGRAM?

In the ever-evolving landscape of social media, TikTok has emerged as a formidable platform with unique features and benefits that set it apart from its counterparts. This bonus chapter will explore the advantages of TikTok compared to other social media platforms, highlighting why it has become a game-changer for individuals and businesses alike.

**1. Algorithmic Magic: Discoverability**

TikTok: TikTok's algorithm is designed to surface content that resonates with users, regardless of the creator's follower count. This means even new users can go viral and gain significant exposure if their content is engaging.

Other Platforms: Platforms like Instagram and Facebook rely heavily on follower count and engagement history, making it harder for new users to get noticed without a substantial following.

## 2. Content Creation and Consumption

TikTok: TikTok's short-form video format encourages quick, creative content. Users can create engaging videos with music, effects, and filters in just a few minutes, making content creation accessible and fun.

Other Platforms: While Instagram has adopted Reels and Facebook Stories, they still emphasize photos and longer-form videos. YouTube focuses on longer content, which requires more time and resources to produce.

## 3. Audience Engagement

TikTok: The platform's design encourages high levels of engagement. Features like duets, stitches, and challenges invite users to interact with each other's content creatively, fostering a sense of community.

Other Platforms: Engagement on platforms like Twitter and Facebook tends to be more passive, with likes, shares, and comments being the primary forms of interaction.

## 4. Trends and Virality

TikTok: TikTok is the epicenter of social media trends. The platform's structure makes it easy for trends to spread rapidly, allowing users to tap into viral content and increase their visibility.

Other Platforms: Trends on Instagram and Facebook often originate from TikTok and tend to spread more slowly. Twitter is a notable exception, where trends can also spread quickly but typically involve text-based content.

### 5. Monetisation Opportunities

TikTok: TikTok offers various monetisation options for creators, including the Creator Fund, brand partnerships, and live gifts. The platform is particularly supportive of influencer marketing.

Other Platforms: YouTube provides significant monetisation opportunities through ad revenue and memberships, while Instagram and Facebook also support brand partnerships. However, monetisation on Twitter is still relatively limited.

### 6. Authenticity and Creativity

TikTok: TikTok values authenticity and creativity. Users are encouraged to be themselves, which fosters a genuine connection with the audience. The platform's tools and features inspire creative expression.

Other Platforms: Instagram often emphasizes aesthetics and polished content, which can sometimes lead to a less authentic user experience. Facebook and Twitter focus more on information sharing and updates.

## 7. Community Building

TikTok: TikTok's algorithmic feed (For You Page) helps build niche communities. Users often find themselves within subcultures and communities that align with their interests, fostering deeper connections.

Other Platforms: Facebook groups and Reddit forums also build communities but often require users to seek out these groups actively. Instagram's community building is usually centered around influencers and their followers.

## 8. Music Integration

TikTok: TikTok's seamless integration with music is one of its standout features. Users can easily add popular songs to their videos, participate in music trends, and even discover new music.

Other Platforms: While Instagram and Facebook have music features, they are not as integral to the platform experience as on TikTok. YouTube supports music but focuses more on video content.

**9. User-Friendly Editing Tools**

TikTok: TikTok offers powerful, user-friendly video editing tools within the app. Users can add effects, transitions, text, and music without needing external software.

Other Platforms: Instagram and Facebook have added more editing tools, but they still lag behind TikTok in terms of ease of use and creative capabilities. YouTube provides advanced editing but typically requires external software.

**10. Global Reach and Cultural Impact**

TikTok: TikTok has a massive global user base and has significantly influenced global pop culture. Its short-form, engaging content appeals to a wide demographic, making it a cultural phenomenon.

Other Platforms: While Facebook and Instagram also have global reach, TikTok's impact on culture and trends, especially among younger audiences, is more pronounced. Twitter influences news and current events but not as much in everyday cultural trends.

**Conclusion: TikTok's Unique Edge**

TikTok's unique combination of an intuitive algorithm, short-form content, high engagement, and creative tools gives it a significant edge over other social media platforms.

It democratises content creation, allowing anyone to go viral and build a community, regardless of their starting point. For businesses and individuals looking to make a mark, TikTok offers an unparalleled opportunity to reach a global audience in a fun, engaging, and authentic way.

As you leverage the power of TikTok, remember to stay true to your unique voice and continuously explore the platform's features to create content that resonates with your audience. Embrace the creativity, enjoy the journey, and watch as your content captures the world's attention.

# DEALING WITH NEGATIVITY

Engaging with your audience is crucial for success on TikTok, but as with any social media platform, not all feedback will be positive. Handling negative comments effectively is essential for maintaining a positive online presence and fostering a supportive community. This chapter will provide strategies for managing and responding to negative comments on TikTok.

**1. Stay Calm and Reflect**

When you receive a negative comment, it's natural to feel defensive or upset. However, it's important to stay calm and take a moment to reflect before responding. Avoid reacting impulsively, as this can escalate the situation.

Tips:

Take a deep breath and give yourself a moment before responding.

Reflect on the comment and try to understand the perspective of the commenter.

Consider whether the comment is constructive criticism or simply trolling.

## 2. Identify the Nature of the Comment

Not all negative comments are the same. It's essential to identify whether the comment is constructive criticism, a genuine complaint, or a troll trying to provoke a reaction. This will help you determine the best way to respond.

Types of Negative Comments:

Constructive Criticism: Offers feedback that can help you improve.

Genuine Complaints: Reflects a real issue or dissatisfaction.

Trolling: Intends to provoke or upset without offering any real value.

## 3. Responding to Constructive Criticism

Constructive criticism, although sometimes hard to hear, can be valuable. Acknowledge the feedback and show appreciation for the commenter's perspective. This demonstrates that you are open to improvement and value your audience's input.

Example Response:

"Thank you for your feedback! I'll keep that in mind for future videos. Your support helps me improve!"

### 4. Addressing Genuine Complaints

If a comment highlights a genuine issue or complaint, it's important to address it promptly and professionally. Apologise if necessary, and offer a solution or explanation to resolve the issue.

Example Response:

"I'm sorry to hear that you had this experience. Please DM me with more details so I can make it right."

### 5. Dealing with Trolls and Harassment

Trolling comments are meant to provoke and disrupt. Engaging with trolls often escalates the situation, so it's best to ignore or block such users. TikTok also provides features to report and block users who post abusive comments.

Tips:

Ignore or delete trolling comments.

Use TikTok's block and report features to manage abusive users.

Avoid feeding the trolls by not responding to provocative comments.

## 6. Setting Boundaries and Moderation

Set clear boundaries for acceptable behavior on your account. Use TikTok's moderation tools to filter out inappropriate comments and maintain a positive environment.

Tips:

Enable comment filters to automatically hide inappropriate comments.

Use keywords to block specific terms or phrases.

Pin a comment to set the tone for engagement on your video.

## 7. Turning Negativity into Positivity

Sometimes, you can turn a negative comment into a positive interaction. Respond with kindness, humour, or a helpful attitude to defuse the situation and show that you can handle criticism gracefully.

Example Response:

"Thank you for your comment! I'll keep trying my best to improve. Appreciate your input!"

8. Encouraging Positive Engagement

Foster a supportive community by encouraging positive interactions and highlighting constructive feedback. Engage with your followers by responding to positive comments and showing appreciation for their support.

Tips:

Highlight and respond to positive comments to reinforce a supportive community.

Encourage your followers to share their thoughts and feedback.

Create a community culture where constructive criticism is valued and trolling is discouraged.

**9. Learning from Negative Feedback**

Negative comments, especially constructive ones, can provide valuable insights into areas for improvement.

Use this feedback to refine your content and approach, ultimately helping you grow as a creator.

Tips:

Regularly review feedback and identify common themes or issues.

Use negative comments as learning opportunities to improve your content.

Keep an open mind and be willing to adapt based on feedback.

## 10. Maintaining Your Mental Health

Dealing with negative comments can be emotionally taxing. It's important to prioritize your mental health and take steps to protect your well-being.

Tips:

Take breaks from social media if you feel overwhelmed.
Surround yourself with supportive friends and family.

Focus on the positive feedback and remember why you started creating content.

**Conclusion**

Negative comments are an inevitable part of being a content creator on TikTok. By handling them with grace and professionalism, you can maintain a positive online presence and foster a supportive community.

Remember to stay calm, identify the nature of the comment, and respond appropriately. Use negative feedback as an opportunity to learn and grow, and don't forget to take care of your mental health. With these strategies, you can navigate the challenges of negative comments and continue to thrive on TikTok.

# FUTURE TRENDS

As the landscape of social media continues to evolve at a rapid pace, staying ahead of future trends is essential for maintaining relevance and maximising impact.

Basically, don't get left behind.

TikTok, being at the forefront of innovation, will undoubtedly shape and be shaped by these trends. This chapter explores the potential future trends for TikTok and social media, offering insights into what to expect and how to prepare.

### 1. Enhanced Augmented Reality (AR) and Virtual Reality (VR)

Trend Overview: AR and VR technologies are set to become more integrated into social media platforms, offering immersive experiences for users.

TikTok's Role: TikTok is likely to expand its AR capabilities, allowing creators to use more sophisticated filters, effects, and virtual environments. Expect to see VR experiences where users can interact with content in a 3D space.

Preparation Tips:

Start experimenting with TikTok's current AR features to become comfortable with the technology.

Stay updated on new AR tools and effects released by TikTok.

Consider how VR experiences can be incorporated into your content strategy.

### 2. Social Commerce Expansion

Trend Overview: Social commerce, where social media platforms serve as direct sales channels, will continue to grow.

TikTok's Role: TikTok's shopping features will likely expand, offering more seamless ways for users to purchase products directly from videos. Live shopping events and in-app stores will become more prevalent.

Preparation Tips:

Integrate shopping links and product tags into your TikTok content.
Participate in live shopping events to engage directly with potential customers.

Collaborate with influencers to promote products through authentic endorsements.

### 3. Personalised Content

Trend Overview: Personalisation will become even more critical, with algorithms delivering highly tailored content to individual users.

TikTok's Role: TikTok's algorithm will continue to refine its ability to deliver personalised content based on user behavior and preferences. This will increase user engagement and satisfaction.

Preparation Tips:

Analyse your audience's preferences and tailor your content accordingly.
Use TikTok's analytics to understand what types of content resonate most with your followers.
Experiment with different formats and topics to see what garners the most engagement.

### 4. Increased Focus on Authenticity

Trend Overview: As users become more discerning, authenticity will be more valued than highly polished, commercial content.

TikTok's Role: TikTok will continue to be a platform where genuine, relatable content thrives. Authenticity in storytelling and interactions will be key to building trust and loyalty.

Preparation Tips:

Share behind-the-scenes content and personal stories to build a connection with your audience.

Engage with your followers through comments, duets, and Q&A sessions.

Focus on creating content that reflects your true self or brand values.

### 5. Short-Form Video Dominance

Trend Overview: Short-form video content will remain dominant, with even more platforms adopting similar formats to TikTok.

TikTok's Role: TikTok will continue to lead the short-form video trend, possibly extending video length while maintaining its quick, engaging format.

Preparation Tips:

Keep your videos concise and engaging, ensuring you capture attention within the first few seconds.

Utilise TikTok's editing tools to create dynamic, fast-paced content.

Stay updated on optimal video lengths as trends evolve.

6. Enhanced Collaboration Features

Trend Overview: Collaboration between creators will become more seamless, with platforms offering enhanced tools for co-creation.

TikTok's Role: TikTok will likely introduce new features to facilitate easier and more creative collaborations between users, such as split-screen options, shared editing, and collaborative playlists.

Preparation Tips:

Seek out collaboration opportunities with other creators in your niche.

Experiment with TikTok's duet and stitch features to create collaborative content.

Engage with your community to build relationships that can lead to future collaborations.

## 7. Focus on Mental Health and Well-being

Trend Overview: As awareness of mental health issues grows, social media platforms will focus more on promoting well-being.

TikTok's Role: TikTok will implement features and campaigns to support mental health, such as break reminders, supportive content, and access to mental health resources.

Preparation Tips:

Create content that promotes mental health and well-being.

Use TikTok's platform to spread awareness about mental health issues.

Engage with TikTok's mental health campaigns and initiatives.

## 8. Integration of AI and Machine Learning

Trend Overview: AI and machine learning will play a more significant role in content creation, curation, and user interaction.

TikTok's Role: TikTok will leverage AI to provide more personalised recommendations, improve content moderation, and offer advanced content creation tools.

Preparation Tips:

Stay informed about new AI tools and features introduced by TikTok.

Experiment with AI-driven content creation tools to enhance your videos.

Use AI analytics to gain deeper insights into your audience and content performance.

## 9. Environmental and Social Responsibility

Trend Overview: Users will increasingly expect brands and creators to be socially and environmentally responsible.

TikTok's Role: TikTok will support and promote content that focuses on sustainability and social issues, encouraging creators to take a stand on important topics.

Preparation Tips:

Share content that highlights your commitment to social and environmental causes.

Participate in TikTok's campaigns related to sustainability and social justice.

Collaborate with other creators and brands that align with your values.

## 10. Advanced Analytics and Insights

Trend Overview: Advanced analytics tools will provide deeper insights into content performance and audience behavior.

TikTok's Role: TikTok will continue to enhance its analytics offerings, giving creators more data to refine their strategies and improve engagement.

Preparation Tips:

Regularly review TikTok analytics to understand your content's performance.

Use insights to make data-driven decisions about your content strategy.

Experiment with different types of content and analyze the results to optimise your approach.

## Conclusion

The future of TikTok and social media is bright,

with exciting trends on the horizon that promise to enhance user experiences and offer new opportunities for creators. By staying informed and adapting to these trends, you can ensure that your content remains relevant, engaging, and impactful.

Embrace the changes, experiment with new features, and continue to connect with your audience in authentic and meaningful ways. With the right approach, you can leverage these future trends to achieve lasting success on TikTok and beyond.

Happy TikToking, and here's to your continued success in the ever-evolving world of social media!

# CONCLUSION

As we draw this book to a close, it's clear that TikTok offers a dynamic and unparalleled platform for sharing ideas, promoting products, and achieving viral success. From the creative spark of a single video to the strategic planning behind a comprehensive marketing campaign, TikTok has transformed the landscape of social media and opened up endless opportunities for businesses and individuals alike.

By now, you should have a wealth of ideas and strategies at your fingertips. We've explored a diverse array of content ideas, from showcasing your company's vision and sharing invaluable business advice to offering practical life hacks and leveraging influencer partnerships.

Each of these concepts is designed to help you connect with your audience in meaningful ways, build your brand's identity, and achieve the kind of engagement that turns casual viewers into loyal fans.

**Embrace the TikTok Spirit**

The key to thriving on TikTok lies in embracing the platform's unique spirit. TikTok thrives on authenticity, creativity, and spontaneity. It's not just about polished, professional videos; it's about real moments, relatable content, and genuine interactions. Your audience is looking for content that resonates with them on a personal level, that entertains, educates, or inspires them in some way. Don't be afraid to experiment, to try new things, and to let your personality shine through in every video.

**Stay Agile and Adapt**

The social media landscape is ever-changing, and TikTok is no exception. Trends come and go, algorithms evolve, and audience preferences shift. Staying agile and adaptable is crucial to maintaining your relevance and success on the platform. Keep an eye on emerging trends, listen to your audience, and be ready to pivot your strategy as needed. Continuous learning and adaptation will keep your content fresh and engaging.

**Engage and Build Community**

At its core, TikTok is a community. It's a place where people come together to share, create, and connect. Building a strong community around your brand should be a primary focus. Engage with your audience by responding to comments, participating in trends, and collaborating with other creators. Foster a sense of belonging and loyalty among your followers by creating content that reflects their interests and values.

**Measure Success and Iterate**

Finally, remember that success on TikTok is a journey, not a destination. Use the platform's analytics tools to measure your performance and gain insights into what works and what doesn't. Pay attention to engagement metrics, viewer demographics, and content performance. Use this data to iterate on your strategy, refining your approach to maximize impact and achieve your goals.

**Your TikTok Journey Awaits**

As you embark on your TikTok journey, keep in mind that the most successful creators and brands are those who stay true to themselves, consistently provide value, and remain responsive to their audience. With the ideas and strategies outlined in this book, you are well-equipped to create compelling content, engage your audience, and make a lasting impact on TikTok.

So, go ahead and unleash your creativity. Whether you're a seasoned marketer or a budding entrepreneur, the possibilities on TikTok are endless. Your journey to viral success starts now. Embrace the adventure, have fun, and watch as your brand reaches new heights.

Thank you for joining us on this journey. We can't wait to see what you create. Happy TikToking!

# ESSENTIAL RESOURCES

As you embark on your TikTok journey, having the right resources at your disposal can make all the difference. From tools for creating and editing content to sources of inspiration and learning, this chapter will provide a comprehensive list of resources to help you achieve TikTok success.

**1. Video Creation and Editing Tools**

TikTok's Built-in Editor

Description: TikTok's own video editor is user-friendly and packed with features like effects, transitions, text overlays, and music integration.
Use: Perfect for quick edits and on-the-go content creation.

Adobe Premiere Rush

Description: A professional video editing app with a simplified interface, suitable for creating polished TikTok videos.
Use: Ideal for users who need more advanced editing features.

InShot

Description: A versatile mobile video editor that allows for trimming, cutting, and merging clips, as well as adding music, filters, and text.
Use: Great for enhancing your videos with professional touches.

CapCut

Description: A popular video editing app by ByteDance (TikTok's parent company) that offers advanced features like keyframe animation, chroma key, and 3D effects.
Use: Best for creating highly stylized and visually compelling videos.

VSCO

Description: Primarily known for photo editing, VSCO also offers robust video editing capabilities with filters and adjustment tools.
Use: Excellent for maintaining a consistent aesthetic across your content.

## 2. Music and Sound Effects

TikTok's Music Library

Description: Access to a vast library of licensed music tracks and sound effects directly within the app.
Use: Essential for keeping your content trendy and engaging.

Epidemic Sound

Description: A subscription-based service providing a wide range of royalty-free music and sound effects.
Use: Ideal for creators looking for high-quality audio without copyright issues.

Soundstripe

Description: Another great source for royalty-free music and sound effects with a subscription model.
Use: Useful for adding unique and professional audio to your videos.

Bensound

Description: Offers free and affordable music tracks for various types of content.
Use: Perfect for creators on a budget needing

background music.

## 3. Graphics and Design Tools

Canva

Description: An easy-to-use design tool for creating graphics, thumbnails, and other visual content.
Use: Great for designing eye-catching cover images and promotional graphics.

Adobe Spark

Description: A suite of design tools for creating social media graphics, short videos, and web pages.
Use: Useful for producing professional-looking visual content with ease.

Over

Description: A mobile app for creating visually appealing graphics and marketing materials.
Use: Ideal for on-the-go content creation and design.

## 4. Analytics and Performance Tracking

TikTok Analytics

Description: Built-in analytics tool available for

TikTok Pro accounts, providing insights into video performance, audience demographics, and trends.

Use: Essential for understanding what works and refining your content strategy.

Hootsuite

Description: A social media management tool that includes analytics for various platforms, including TikTok.

Use: Useful for managing and analyzing your overall social media presence.

Analisa.io

Description: A TikTok analytics tool that offers in-depth insights into account performance, engagement rates, and follower growth.

Use: Ideal for tracking and benchmarking your progress.

Social Blade

Description: A platform that provides analytics for TikTok and other social media channels, including follower growth and engagement statistics.

Use: Helpful for monitoring your TikTok metrics

over time.

## 5. Learning and Inspiration

TikTok Creator Portal

Description: TikTok's official resource center for creators, offering tutorials, best practices, and tips.

Use: Essential for staying updated with platform features and improving your content creation skills.

YouTube Tutorials

Description: A wealth of video tutorials from various creators on TikTok strategies, editing tips, and trend analysis.

Use: Great for visual learners looking to enhance their TikTok expertise.

Online Courses

Description: Platforms like Udemy, Skillshare, and Coursera offer courses on social media marketing, video editing, and content creation.

Use: Perfect for structured learning and gaining comprehensive knowledge.

Industry Blogs

Description: Blogs like Social Media Examiner, HubSpot, and Later provide insights, tips, and trend analyses.
Use: Useful for staying informed about the latest in social media marketing.

## 6. Community and Networking

TikTok Communities

Description: Join TikTok creator communities and groups on platforms like Reddit, Facebook, and LinkedIn to connect with other creators.

Use: Valuable for networking, sharing tips, and finding collaboration opportunities.

Creator Meetups

Description: Attend virtual or in-person meetups and events for TikTok creators.

Use: Excellent for networking, learning, and growing your influence.

Mentorship Programs

Description: Seek out mentorship programs or find a

mentor within your industry.

Use: Beneficial for personalized guidance and growth.

**Conclusion**

Equipped with these resources, you are now ready to take your TikTok content to the next level. From powerful editing tools and royalty-free music libraries to comprehensive analytics platforms and learning resources, these tools will help you create high-quality, engaging videos that resonate with your audience. Remember, the key to success on TikTok is to stay creative, be consistent, and continually learn and adapt. With the right resources and a strategic approach, you can harness the full potential of TikTok to achieve your goals.

# THE END

www.ingramcontent.com/pod-product-compliance
Lightning Source LLC
Chambersburg PA
CBHW031420210526
45464CB00005B/1978